CREMATION & CATHOLIC BURIAL

A GUIDE FOR FAMILIES

CREMATION & CATHOLIC BURIAL

A GUIDE FOR FAMILIES

JOSHUA R. LEBLANC

© 2025 by Joshua R. LeBlanc
All rights reserved.

No part of this publication may be reproduced, distributed, or transmitted in any form or by any means, including photocopying, recording, or other electronic or mechanical methods, without the prior written permission of the publisher, except in the case of brief quotations embodied in critical reviews and certain other noncommercial uses permitted by copyright law.

For permission requests, contact:
Bayou State Publishing
P.O. Box 1049
Abbeville, LA 70511
Email: info@bayoustatepublishing.com
Website: bayoustatepublishing.com

ISBN: 978-1-970659-03-0

Printed in the United States of America
First Edition, 2025

Published by **Bayou State Publishing**
Youngsville, LA

Disclaimer:
The information contained in this book is provided for general educational and informational purposes only. Nothing in this book should be construed as, or relied upon as, legal advice. Laws and regulations vary by jurisdiction and are subject to change. Readers are strongly encouraged to consult with a qualified attorney before making any decisions or taking any action based on the material presented herein. The author and publisher expressly disclaim any liability for actions taken or not taken based on the contents of this book.

ABOUT THE AUTHOR

Joshua R. LeBlanc serves as the Executive Director of Holy Family Cemetery in New Iberia, Louisiana. He was ordained a Catholic deacon for the Diocese of Lafayette in 2016 and is currently assigned to St. Martin de Tours Catholic Church in St. Martinville.

Deacon LeBlanc brings a unique combination of theological insight, pastoral care, and administrative precision to the sacred work of cemetery management.

He holds a Master of Arts in Moral Theology and a +30 in Bioethics from Holy Apostles College and Seminary and is certified in Bioethics by the National Catholic Bioethics Center. He is currently pursuing a Doctorate in the field of Bioethics.

In addition to his ministry and administrative leadership, Deacon LeBlanc is a commissioned Civil Law Notary Public in and for the State of Louisiana and the owner of two small businesses — an IT firm and Chesterton's Fine Cigars in Youngsville, La. It is through this background that he shares his expertise in faith, ethics, and cemetery law.

Deacon LeBlanc also serves as a police chaplain and reserve police officer for the Youngsville and Abbeville Police Departments. He is also chaplain for the Military and Hospitaller Order of St. Lazarus of Jerusalem in the rank of Ecclesiastical Commander, whose mission is to serve the sick and dying. He is the Delegate for the Imperial

Calcasieu Delegation and Vice Chancellor for Communications for the Grand Priory of America

As a deacon, he has ministered to grieving families for years, guiding them through the Catholic Church's teachings on death, burial, and resurrection. As a professional cemetery administrator, he has developed robust compliance systems rooted in Louisiana law, ensuring that every interment, fund, and record upholds both the dignity of the deceased and the legal obligations of the living.

Deacon LeBlanc is the author of *The Louisiana Cemetery Handbook: Law, Compliance, and Administration* and *The Louisiana Cemetery Form Book: Legal Documents, Templates, and Compliance Tools for Cemetery Authorities and Notaries Public*, the companion books in this series. Together, these works form the foundation of *The Louisiana Cemetery Authority Series*, a comprehensive legal and operational reference for religious and civil cemetery professionals throughout the state.

He and his wife, Annie, reside in Abbeville, Louisiana, with their cat Benedict.

TABLE OF CONTENTS

Introduction 1

Chapter 1:
Why the Church Cares for the Body After Death 5

Chapter 2:
The Catholic Understanding of Death and Resurrection 9

Chapter 3:
Cremation in the Catholic Church — What Is Permitted? 15

Chapter 4:
Why Cremated Remains Must Be Interred 21

Chapter 5:
Why Keeping Remains at Home Is Not Recommended 29

Chapter 6:
Why Scattering Cremated Remains Is Not Permitted 37

Chapter 7:
The Catholic Funeral Rites with Cremation 43

Chapter 8:
Choosing a Resting Place — Burial, Mausoleum, Niche 49

Chapter 9:
Memorialization and Catholic Tradition 59

Chapter 10:
Common Questions Families Ask (Pastoral Q&A) 65

Chapter 11:
A Step-by-Step Guide for Families Bringing Remains for Burial 73

Chapter 12:
Conclusion — A Final Word of Faith, Hope, and Love 81

General Index 85

INTRODUCTION

Why This Book Exists

The death of someone we love is one of the most painful and confusing moments in life. Families suddenly face decisions they never expected to make — decisions about funeral arrangements, cremation, burial, memorials, and the future. In the midst of grief, these choices can feel overwhelming. Many families today choose cremation without fully understanding what the Catholic Church teaches or why the Church insists that the cremated remains of a loved one must be interred in sacred ground.

This booklet was written to offer clarity, comfort, and guidance.

It exists for families — especially those who carry the weight of loss — who want to do what is loving, faithful, and dignified for someone dear to them. It exists for grandchildren who inherit an urn they don't know what to do with, for adult children who kept their parents' ashes out of grief, for spouses who delayed burial because they weren't ready to let go, and for families who simply want to understand what the Church asks of them.

Most of all, this booklet exists to help families see the beauty behind the Church's teaching.

The Catholic Church has always cared deeply for the bodies of the dead. This care comes from a profound truth: the human body is not just a shell or container — it is part of the person God created, loved, redeemed, and will one day raise from the dead. Whether a person is buried in a casket or cremated and placed in an urn, their body remains sacred. The rituals, prayers, and teachings of the Church all flow from that truth.

Cremation is permitted. But the Church also teaches that the cremated remains must be interred in a cemetery, mausoleum, or columbarium. This is not merely a rule — it is an act of love. Burial proclaims our belief in the resurrection, gives families a place to pray, protects the remains from loss or neglect, and provides the gentle closure the human heart needs to heal. Interment is a final gift to the one who has died, and a source of peace for the living.

Whether you are preparing for the future, making decisions today, or seeking to honor someone whose remains are already at home, this booklet will walk with you step by step. It will explain what the Church teaches, why those teachings matter, and how you can provide the sacred resting place your loved one deserves.

May this guide be a source of hope, clarity, and consolation for you.

May it help you entrust those you love into the hands of God, who is faithful in life, faithful in death, and faithful forever.

EXPLANATION OF ABBREVIATIONS USED IN THIS BOOK

Throughout this booklet, several commonly used Catholic and ecclesial documents are referenced in parentheses to help families locate the source of various teachings. Here is a simple guide to what they mean:

CCC – Catechism of the Catholic Church

A universal summary of Catholic teaching on faith, morals, and the sacraments.

CIC – Code of Canon Law

The Church's universal law, including the norms governing funerals, cemeteries, and cremation.

OCF – Order of Christian Funerals

The official liturgical book containing the Vigil, Funeral Mass, and Rite of Committal.

CDF – Congregation for the Doctrine of the Faith

(renamed in 2022 as the Dicastery for the Doctrine of the Faith)
The Vatican office responsible for doctrinal documents, including the instruction on cremation.

Ad resurgendum cum Christo

A 2016 instruction issued by the CDF that explains the Church's norms for cremation and the proper treatment of cremated remains.

Piam et Constantem

A 1963 instruction that first permitted cremation under certain conditions, laying the foundation for the discipline we follow today.

Scripture Citations (e.g., John 11:25, 1 Thess 4:13–18)

Biblical passages that illustrate the Christian understanding of death and resurrection.

These abbreviations are included sparingly and only where helpful. They are provided not to overwhelm but to give families confidence that the Church's teaching is rooted in Scripture, tradition, and the authoritative wisdom of the Church.

CHAPTER 1

A Christian View of Death: Faith, Hope, and the Dignity of the Human Body

Death is one of the most difficult moments a family can face. When someone we love dies, our hearts struggle to make sense of the loss, the change, and the ache that follows. Yet from the beginning of Christianity, believers have understood death not as the end of life but as the doorway into eternal life with God. The Christian faith transforms how we see death, how we mourn, and how we honor the body of someone we love.

Death Is Not the End

In the Gospel, Jesus reveals that death does not have the final word. He stands at the tomb of His friend Lazarus. He proclaims, "I am the resurrection and the life. Whoever believes in Me, though he die, yet shall he live" (John 11:25). This promise is the foundation of the Church's teaching on death: we believe in the resurrection of the body and life everlasting.

Because of this hope, Christians do not treat death as the end. We do not see it as the disappearance of a person into nothing. Instead, we view it as the moment when the soul returns to God, who created and loved that person from the first moment of existence.

The Sacredness of the Human Body

Catholics believe that the body is not merely a vessel that we use during our earthly lives. The body is an essential part of who we are as human beings. Through baptism, the body becomes a temple of the Holy Spirit (1 Corinthians 6:19; Catechism of the Catholic Church [CCC] 364–365). With sacred chrism, it is sealed for Christ. Through the Holy Eucharist, the body is nourished by the very Body and Blood of the Lord who died at Calvary. The human body is the visible expression of a person made in the image and likeness of God – the *Imago Dei!*

Even after death, the body retains its sacred dignity. This is why the Church has always shown respect and care for the dead. The body is prepared with reverence; prayers accompany the family; the deceased is laid to rest with dignity; the community gathers to commend the soul to God.

This reverence does not end simply because a person's soul has left the body. The body remains the earthly sign of a beloved child of God who awaits the resurrection. This belief is the foundation for the Church's teachings about burial and cremation.

Following Christ in Death and Burial

When Jesus died, His body was reverently prepared, wrapped in linen, and laid in a tomb. His followers treated His body with care, devotion, and love. The Church continues this tradition when she buries her faithful, because Christians are united with Christ in life, in death, and in resurrection.

Every human body — whether intact or cremated — deserves a share in that same dignity and sacred rest. Catholic burial practices imitate Christ's burial and proclaim belief in His rising.

A Community of Faith and Love

Death never affects just one person; it touches the entire community. Families, friends, and parish members come together to pray, support one another, and accompany the deceased with the rites of the Church. Burial is part of this communal act of love. It places the person within the larger family of faith, alongside generations who have gone before and generations who will come after.

Cemeteries themselves are sacred places — places of memory, prayer, and hope. They remind us that Christians rest in the peace of Christ, waiting for the day He will raise them up.

The Christian Meaning of Mourning

When we lose someone we love, grief is natural and holy. Jesus Himself wept at the tomb of Lazarus. But grief is transformed by the hope we have in God's mercy. Christian mourning is not despair; it is the tender ache of love that trusts in God's promise.

The funeral rites of the Church exist not only to honor the deceased but also to surround the living with consolation. The prayers, readings, and rituals speak of hope, mercy, and resurrection. They place our grief within the story of Christ's victory over death.

Why This Booklet?

In today's world, many people are unsure of what the Church teaches about death, cremation, and burial. Families may be uncertain about what to do with cremated remains or why the Church asks that they be interred. This booklet is meant to offer clarity, compassion, and guidance. Above all, it is meant to help families honor their loved ones in a way that reflects the beauty of our faith and the dignity of the human person.

For Catholics, how we treat the body in death proclaims what we believe about life. With that foundation, we now turn to the history of Christian burial and how it shapes the Church's teaching today.

CHAPTER 2

Why Catholics Historically Preferred Burial

For nearly two thousand years, Christians have expressed their faith in the resurrection by burying their dead. While today the Church permits cremation under certain conditions, burial remains the traditional and preferred practice because it carries deep theological, spiritual, and historical meaning.

Understanding why Christians overwhelmingly chose burial throughout the centuries helps families appreciate the Catholic approach to death — and illuminates the Church's teaching about the dignity owed to human remains.

The Early Christians and Pagan Cremation

To understand Christian burial practices, it helps to look at the world in which Christianity was born.

In the ancient Roman Empire, cremation was extremely common — but it was tied to beliefs very different from the Gospel. Many pagan cultures practiced cremation because they did not believe in a bodily resurrection. They saw the body as disposable, temporary, or even irrelevant to the soul's destiny (cf. Tertullian, De Resurrectione Carnis, ch. 1–3).

Christians, however, proclaimed something astonishing and new – The body will rise again.

Because of this belief, early Christians rejected the cremation customs of the surrounding culture. They wanted their burial practices to reflect the truth revealed in Christ — that the body is good, holy, and destined for eternal life.

Early Christian writings, inscriptions, and archaeological evidence show overwhelmingly that believers buried their dead, preserving the body as a witness to hope.

Christ's Burial Is the Model for Christian Burial

Jesus Himself was buried in a tomb. His followers received His body, wrapped it with reverence, anointed it with spices, and laid it in the earth. (cf. John 19:38–42; CCC 1683)

This sacred act taught the early Church that burial imitates Christ.

To bury the dead is to honor them as He was honored.
To lay someone in a tomb or grave is to follow the path Christ sanctified by His own Body.

For Christians, burial has never been merely a cultural custom — it is a statement of faith in the Resurrection of Jesus Christ (CCC 2300–2301).

The Body Is a Temple of the Holy Spirit

Christians have always believed that the body is not an empty shell. It is the visible sign of the person, created in God's image.

- Baptism sanctifies the body.
- The anointings of Confirmation and the Anointing of the Sick bless the body.
- The Eucharist nourishes our own body with the Body of Christ.

For these reasons, the body retains its dignity even after death. Early Christians believed the body should be laid to rest gently and reverently, awaiting the resurrection of the last day.

This belief naturally led to burial.

The Rise of Christian Cemeteries

Christian burial places — eventually called "cemeteries" — developed early in the life of the Church. The word "cemetery" comes from the Greek *koimeterion*, meaning "a sleeping place." (cf. OCF Glossary) This name itself is a proclamation of Christian hope: in death, the body sleeps in peace until Christ awakens it.

Cemeteries soon became:

- Places of prayer
- Places of community
- Places of memory
- Places where the faithful were gathered together in hope

Families visited graves, prayed for their loved ones, and celebrated the Communion of Saints. Many martyrs and saints were buried in tombs that became sites of devotion.

The cemetery was — and remains — a sacred space where believers express love, grief, hope, and faith (Order of Christian Funerals [OCF] 27–29).

Burial as a Communion of Families and Generations

Christians saw burial as a way of preserving family connections across generations. Whole families were buried together, creating physical reminders of the unity of the human family in Christ.

Graves and tombs also served as a testimony to future generations:

- A place to pray
- A place to remember
- A place to pass on the story of a person's life

Burial in consecrated ground ensured that the faithful remained connected to the Church even in death.

Why This Tradition Still Matters Today

Even though cremation is now allowed, the Church's preference for burial has not changed. Burial continues to make visible the Christian belief in:

- The sacredness of the human body
- The hope of the resurrection
- The connection between the living and the dead
- The importance of a permanent resting place
- The communal nature of grieving and remembrance

The Church's teachings about cremation — including why cremated remains must still be interred — grow directly out of this ancient and sacred tradition.

Burial is not only a respectful practice — it is a testimony of the faith we profess.

Looking Ahead

Now that we have explored the history and meaning of Christian burial, we turn to a question many families face today:

> **What exactly does the Catholic Church teach about cremation?**

CHAPTER 3

What the Catholic Church Teaches About Cremation

Cremation has become increasingly common in recent decades, and many families today are unsure what the Church teaches or how to approach the decision. While the Catholic Church now permits cremation, it does so with important conditions meant to preserve the dignity of the human body and the truth of the resurrection.

This chapter explains clearly and simply what the Church teaches — so that families can make informed, faithful, and reverent choices.

The Church's Teaching Has Developed — Not Changed in Meaning

For most of Christian history, cremation was discouraged or forbidden because it was often associated with beliefs contrary to Christianity — especially the denial of the resurrection of the body.

In 1963, the Church began permitting cremation under certain conditions, recognizing changing cultural and practical realities. This permission was formally incorporated into canon law and the Church's liturgical books (Instruction Piam et Constantem, 1963).

However, what has remained constant is the core teaching:

> **The human body must be treated with dignity, even after death, and cremated remains must receive the same reverence and honor as a full body.**

The meaning has not changed; the pastoral application has.

The Church's Official Teaching

The most direct, authoritative teachings on cremation come from:

- The *Code of Canon Law* (canons 1176 – 1185)
- The *Order of Christian Funerals*
- The Vatican's 2016 instruction *Ad resurgendum cum Christo*

Together, these sources make the Church's position clear.

Here are the essential points in plain, family-friendly language:

Cremation is permitted.

Catholics may choose cremation as long as it is not selected for reasons contrary to Christian doctrine (CIC, can. 1176 §3).

Examples of unacceptable reasons would be:

- Denying the resurrection of the body
- Rejecting Christian teaching about the dignity of the body
- Choosing cremation out of hatred or contempt for the Church or faith

Cremated remains must be treated as the body of a human person.

The Church insists that cremated remains be:

- Handled with reverence
- Kept intact
- Placed in a proper vessel
- Interred in a sacred place (CDF, Ad resurgendum cum Christo, 5–6)

Cremated remains are not objects, mementos, or keepsakes. They are the earthly remains of a beloved child of God.

Cremation should preferably occur *after* the Funeral Mass.

The Church expresses a strong preference — when possible — that the body be present during the Funeral Mass (OCF 129–131). Why?

- The body is the visible sign of the person.
- The rituals were designed to honor the body itself.
- The presence of the body helps families in their grieving.

If circumstances require cremation before the funeral, the Church still permits the Mass with the cremated remains present.

Cremated remains must be interred in a cemetery or sacred place.

This is perhaps the most important point:

Cremated remains must be buried in the ground or entombed in a mausoleum or columbarium.

They may not be:

- Kept at home
- Scattered
- Divided among the family
- Placed in jewelry
- Stored indefinitely
- Kept in a non-sacred place

These practices are prohibited because they separate the remains from the Christian community and do not reflect the dignity owed to the human body.

Catholic burial is still required.

Even with cremation, the Church requires:

- A sacred resting place
- A record of burial
- Prayers for the deceased
- A place for the faithful to visit, remember, and pray

In other words, the basic meaning of Catholic burial remains unchanged.

The Church's Reasoning: Faith and Love

The Catholic teaching on cremation isn't about rules for the sake of rules – It is about what we believe as Catholics.

We believe in the resurrection of the body.

What we do with the body expresses what we believe about it. Interment proclaims the Christian hope that God will raise the dead.

We believe the body is sacred.

The body belongs in a place of reverence — consecrated ground — surrounded by prayer.

We believe grief should be healed, not prolonged.

Keeping remains at home often arises from deep grief, but it can unintentionally delay healing. Burial allows the family to entrust their loved one to God.

We believe in the communion of saints and the unity of the faithful.

A cemetery or columbarium connects the deceased with the broader community of believers.

What This Means for Families

The Church's teaching is not meant to burden families but to guide them toward what is holy, healing, and faithful. If cremation is chosen, the Church asks families to:

- Treat the remains with reverence
- Use a proper urn
- Bring the remains to the parish or cemetery for burial
- Provide a permanent resting place where prayer can continue

By doing these things, families both honor the dignity of their loved one and give public witness to the Christian faith.

Looking Ahead

Now that we understand what the Church teaches about cremation, the next chapter will answer a crucial question:

> **Why does the Church require cremated remains to be interred?**

Chapter 4 will explain the theological, pastoral, and spiritual significance and rationale, as well as the human importance of choosing burial over preserving or scattering remains.

CHAPTER 4

Why Cremated Remains Must Be Interred: Faith, Dignity, and the Hope of Resurrection

For many families today, cremation feels simpler or more practical than traditional burial, and the question naturally arises:

> *If we choose cremation, why does the Church still require the remains to be buried or placed in a sacred space?*

> **Why is keeping them at home or scattering them not permitted? Why does the Church insist on a permanent, consecrated resting place?**

The answer is profoundly beautiful:

Because the human body matters.

It mattered to God when He created it; it mattered in life; it matters in death; and it will matter at the resurrection.

This chapter explains — not with legalism, but with love —why the Church asks families to provide a sacred, permanent resting place for cremated remains.

Cremated Remains Are the Body of a Person, Not "Ashes"

A person's cremated remains are not like fireplace ash or household dust. They are the final earthly remains of someone created in the image and likeness of God, loved by their family, and redeemed by Christ (CDF, Ad resurgendum cum Christo, 6).

Even in cremated form, the Church says:

- The person's identity remains connected to these remains.
- The remains must be treated with the same reverence given to a full body.
- The remains deserve a place of honor, not storage or dispersion.

When families handle cremated remains with dignity, they proclaim a deep truth:

> **This person is sacred. This person's body matters. This person will rise again.**

Burial Proclaims Our Faith in the Resurrection

Burial — whether of a body or cremated remains — makes visible what we believe — that the body will be raised by God on the last day (1 Thessalonians 4:13 – 18; John 5:28 – 29).

A permanent resting place is a testimony to this hope. It says to the world:

- Death is not the end.
- The person is not forgotten.
- God is not finished with their body.
- We await the resurrection with confidence and love.

When remains are scattered or kept at home, this proclamation becomes obscured. Scattering suggests the person simply "returns to nature," while keeping the urn in a house suggests the body no longer needs a sacred resting place. Burial keeps the Christian meaning clear.

A Sacred Place for Prayer and Memory

A grave or niche is more than a physical location. It is:

- A place of prayer
- A place of remembrance
- A place of peace
- A place where family history is preserved
- A place that expresses love long after the funeral
- A place of connection for future generations

A permanent resting place allows children, grandchildren, and great-grandchildren to know where their family came from and to honor the memory of those who came before them (OCF 27; CIC, can. 1240).

When remains are scattered, divided, or kept privately, this connection is lost. There is no shared place of remembrance, no physical spot where a family can gather, pray, and remember.

Burial Protects the Remains from Future Loss, Damage, or Disrespect

Families often do not anticipate the long-term consequences of keeping remains at home. As time passes:

- A family may move.
- A relative inherits the home and does not know what to do with the urn.
- The urn may be placed in a closet, garage, or storage unit.
- Remains can be lost, forgotten, or even discarded through neglect or error.

Cemeteries and columbaria exist to protect the dignity of the remains forever. They preserve memory, prevent loss, and ensure that a person's resting place is treated with respect for generations to come.

A sacred resting place protects the remains as a gift entrusted to the whole Christian community — not a burden placed on a single family member.

Scattering or Dividing Remains Harms the Integrity of the Person

The Church teaches clearly that cremated remains must be kept together, intact, and undivided. They are not something to be shared, separated, or incorporated into objects (CDF, Ad resurgendum cum Christo, 7).

This is because:

- Human remains are sacred.
- A person's identity should not be fragmented.
- The unity of the person should be reflected in the unity of their remains.

Scattering removes the remains from the Christian community and eliminates any place for prayer. Dividing remains treats the body as an object rather than as a sacred whole.

Placing remains into jewelry, artwork, or household items is especially prohibited because it blurs the line between honoring a loved one and wearing or displaying their remains in ways inconsistent with Christian reverence. The body of a loved one is not a possession of ours but rather that of God.

Interment Helps Families Heal and Let Go in a Healthy Way

Often, families keep remains at home because they are not ready emotionally to part with their loved one. This is an understandable, tender response to grief. But over time, keeping remains at home can:

- Prevent full mourning
- Create emotional distress
- Place a quiet burden on the family
- Make it harder to accept the reality of death
- Leave future generations unsure what to do

Interment, by contrast:

- Allows the family to entrust their loved one to God
- Creates a sense of completion and peace

- Provides a sacred place to visit
- Gently guides the grieving toward healing
- Offers a ritual of closure, prayer, and love

The act of placing the remains in sacred ground is not abandonment — it is an act of profound faith and trust (OCF 204–205).

Being Laid to Rest Among the Faithful

The Church believes deeply in the Communion of Saints —the mysterious but real union between the living, the departed, and the saints in heaven.

Interring cremated remains in a Catholic cemetery or columbarium expresses this communion beautifully. The deceased rests:

- Among fellow believers
- In consecrated ground
- Under the care of the Church
- Surrounded by prayer
- In a place set apart for sacred rest

A cemetery is a visible reminder that we journey to God together — not alone.

Burial Is an Act of Love, Faith, and Hope

Choosing to bury cremated remains is not simply obeying a rule. It is an act of:

- Love, because we honor our loved one's dignity
- Faith, because we proclaim belief in the resurrection
- Hope, because we trust God to raise the body on the last day
- Healing, because we entrust the person into God's care
- Witness, because we show the world what we believe as Catholics

When a family brings their loved one to the Church for interment, they are saying:

"Lord, we entrust them to You.
We await the day You make all things new."

This is one of the most beautiful acts a Catholic family can make.

Looking Ahead

Now that we understand *why* cremated remains must be interred, the next chapter will address a common question:

> **"If the Church doesn't allow keeping remains at home, why not? What makes that different?"**

Chapter 5 will examine and explain why burial is necessary

CHAPTER 5

Why Keeping Ashes at Home Is Not Appropriate

Many families keep cremated remains at home out of love, grief, or uncertainty about what to do next. This choice almost always comes from a place of good intentions: a deep desire to stay close to someone who has died. While the Church understands this emotional instinct, she gently teaches that keeping remains at home is not the proper way to honor someone who has died.

This chapter explains *why* — not to judge or shame — but to help families understand the spiritual, emotional, and practical reasons behind the Church's teaching. The Church accompanies families tenderly, offering both compassion and guidance toward what is holy, dignified, and healing.

A Home Is a Place for the Living, Not the Dead

The home is a sacred place — but it is sacred for the living. A home is where:

- Family life unfolds
- Children grow
- Meals are shared

- Prayer and love are lived out daily

But it is not a sacred place of permanent rest. (CIC, can. 1177).

Catholic tradition teaches that the dead belong in a place set apart — consecrated ground — where they can rest in peace and where the community of faith can pray for them. A house, no matter how loving, is temporary. People move, sell property, downsize, or pass away. Homes change hands; cemeteries do not.

Placing cremated remains in the home unintentionally removes the person from the community of believers and the sacred space the Church provides for the dead.

Emotional Burdens on the Family

Families often keep remains at home because they are not ready to let go. This is understandable. Yet over time, the presence of cremated remains in the home can create emotional and spiritual challenges (OCF 4 – 7).

Grief May Be Prolonged

Keeping remains in the home can unintentionally:

- Delay the emotional acceptance of death
- Prevent the family from fully grieving
- Make it harder to entrust the deceased to God

Burial allows families to complete the circle of love and release, trusting God's mercy and care.

The Urn Becomes a Silent Weight

Many families eventually feel uncomfortable with cremated remains in the house, but do not know how to move forward. The urn can become:

- A quiet emotional burden
- A reminder of unresolved grief
- A source of tension among family members
- An obligation passed on to children

Interment lifts that burden from the home and places the loved one in sacred care.

The Future Problem: "Who Will Take Care of the Urn?"

This is one of the most common and painful concerns.

When remains are kept at home:

- Someone must be responsible
- If that person passes away, remains may be forgotten or misplaced (Pastoral note, USCCB Committee on Divine Worship)
- Family members may not agree on what to do
- The urn can be packed away, lost, or even accidentally discarded
- Younger generations may not feel connected to the deceased

Over time, good intentions may crumble under practical realities.

Burial eliminates these dilemmas. It ensures:

- The remains are protected
- A clear record of interment
- A place for future generations to visit
- Peace of mind for the entire family

Keeping Remains at Home Blurs the Line Between Sacred and Ordinary

The Catholic Church teaches that the body — even in cremated form — is sacred. It is not simply memorabilia or something to be stored among everyday objects.

When remains are kept at home, it becomes easy for them to be:

- Placed on a shelf
- Stored in a closet
- Moved from room to room
- Handled without ritual or reverence
- Treated unintentionally as an object instead of human remains

Over time, even in loving families, the sense of sacredness can be diminished.

A cemetery or columbarium restores that sacred space. It sets the remains apart as holy, treating them with the dignity every human being deserves.

A Home Does Not Provide a Place for the Community to Pray

Catholic funerals and burials are never just private events. They are acts of the entire Church.

When remains are kept at home:

- Friends and extended family have no place to visit
- The parish cannot offer communal prayer at the grave
- The deceased is separated from the community of saints
- The person's memory becomes limited to whoever possesses the urn

But when remains are interred:

- Anyone can visit the grave
- The parish can offer the Burial Rites of the Church
- Memorial Masses, All Souls' Day prayers, and blessings occur
- The person is remembered in a public, communal, prayerful way

Cemeteries are visible signs of the Church's love for her dead.

Proper Interment Honors the Body's Final Journey

The Catholic tradition sees life as a pilgrimage — from birth to baptism, to the Eucharist, to the moment we return to God. Burial is the final step in this sacred journey on earth.

Keeping remains at home interrupts this spiritual path, leaving the person's story unresolved in a way the Church sees as incomplete.

Interment completes the journey:

- The body is entrusted to God
- The community commends the soul to His mercy
- The grave becomes a place of hope and prayer
- The story of the person's life finds its proper close

This is why the Church speaks so strongly and lovingly about the need for burial.

The Church Welcomes Families Who Want to Do the Right Thing

Sometimes families worry that they will be judged if they bring remains that have been at home for many years. But the Church's message is always the same:

It is never too late to do the right and holy thing.

Priests, deacons, and cemetery staff gladly assist families with:

- A dignified transfer of remains
- The Rite of Committal
- Help choosing a burial or niche option
- Pastoral care and prayer

The Church's desire is not to scold but to heal, guide, and bring peace.

Looking Ahead

Next, we turn to one of the most misunderstood questions:

> **Why does the Church prohibit scattering cremated remains?**

Chapter 6 will explain this answer in detail.

CHAPTER 6

Why Scattering Cremated Remains Is Not Permitted

In recent years, scattering cremated remains has become a widespread cultural practice. Movies, television, and social media often portray scattering as a beautiful or symbolic gesture — releasing a loved one into the wind, the water, or a meaningful place.

Because of this cultural influence, many families understandably wonder why the Catholic Church prohibits scattering cremated remains. The answer is rooted not in legalism, but in profound truths about the human person, the meaning of the body, and the hope of the resurrection.

Scattering Suggests the Person Has "Disappeared" Rather Than Awaits Resurrection

When remains are scattered, they no longer have a particular resting place. They become part of the environment — air, water, or soil — symbolizing, intentionally or not, that the person is dissolved into nature (CDF, Ad resurgendum cum Christo, 3–4).

But this directly contradicts our faith.

The Church believes:

- The person is unique and unrepeatable
- The body retains its meaning, even in cremated form
- God will raise the body on the last day

Scattering expresses the opposite idea — that the person has simply ceased to exist as a body.

The Church wants every Christian to rest in a place that proclaims hope in the resurrection, not disappearance.

Scattering Removes the Remains from the Community of Faith

Catholic burial is not just about the deceased — it is about the entire Church (CIC, can. 1176 §2).

When remains are scattered:

- There is no grave to visit
- No place for the family to gather and pray
- No site for future generations to remember
- No physical connection to the community or parish
- No sacred ground consecrated for rest

The person becomes *nowhere* when they should be *somewhere* — in a place the Church guards, remembers, and blesses.

A cemetery is more than geography. It is a spiritual home.

Scattering Breaks the Unity of the Body

The Church teaches that cremated remains must remain intact, undivided, and placed together in one sacred place. This is because:

- A person's identity is not something to fragment
- The human body, even in cremated form, is sacred
- The unity of the person must be reflected in the unity of their remains

Scattering or dividing remains contradicts this sacred unity. The body becomes dispersed or broken apart — not what the Church believes honors the dignity of the person.

Scattering Often Expresses a Belief Incompatible With Christianity

The Vatican's document *Ad resurgendum cum Christo* explains that scattering is prohibited because it often expresses views rooted in philosophies or spiritualities that conflict with Christian truth (CDF, Ad resurgendum cum Christo, 3).

These may include:

- Pantheism ("the person becomes part of the universe")
- New Age beliefs ("the spirit is absorbed into nature")
- Nihilism ("the person simply disappears")
- Romantic symbolism without reference to God or resurrection

While families may not intend these meanings, the act itself can symbolically communicate them. The Church wants burial practices to align with Christian belief, not cultural symbolism.

Scattering Removes the Opportunity for Ongoing Prayer and Memory

One of the greatest gifts the Church offers is ongoing prayer for the dead.

When remains are scattered:

- The family loses a place to visit
- Loved ones cannot gather for anniversaries, birthdays, or All Souls' Day
- Children and grandchildren lose the chance to know where their ancestor rests
- The parish community cannot bless or pray at the grave
- The person is forgotten more easily over generations

A sacred resting place preserves the memory of the person for decades — and sometimes centuries — allowing their family and the Church to continue praying for them.

Scattering Can Lead to Accidental Disrespect

Even when done with love, scattering can unintentionally result in:

- Remains being carried away by wind onto unintended places
- Remains washing away, being trampled, or becoming inaccessible
- Remains being spread in public areas where others may walk, play, or discard trash

Over time, the location may be developed, sold, or altered. A place that once felt meaningful may later become inaccessible, commercialized, or destroyed (Pastoral guidelines, USCCB, Cremation & Christian Burial).

Cemeteries ensure that remains remain undisturbed, respected, and protected.

The Church Offers a More Beautiful Way

The Catholic Church does not forbid scattering to be strict or unfeeling. Instead, she offers something richer and more stable: a sacred place of Christian hope.

When remains are interred, the family receives:

- A physical place of connection
- A permanent legacy
- A resting place surrounded by prayer
- The ability to visit on anniversaries and holy days

- The peace of knowing their loved one is cared for always

Scattering cannot offer these things — interment can.

"But They Loved the Lake…" A Gentle Word for Families

Sometimes families choose scattering because the deceased loved a particular place — the ocean, a campsite, the mountains, a lake. These emotions are real and meaningful.

But the Church invites families to honor that memory in ways consistent with faith:

- Visit the place and pray there
- Create a memorial bench, stone, or plaque
- Share stories and memories at that location
- Bring a small amount of soil, water, or sand to the grave as a symbol

These expressions preserve the connection without scattering remains.

Looking Ahead

Now that we have explained why scattering is not permitted, we turn to the next sections of the booklet:

How Catholic funeral rites work when cremation is chosen, and how families can provide a proper final resting place.

CHAPTER 7

The Catholic Funeral Rites with Cremation

When a loved one dies, families often feel overwhelmed by decisions and unsure about the next steps. Whether a family chooses traditional burial or cremation, the Catholic Church provides a beautiful set of funeral rites meant to honor the deceased, comfort the grieving, and proclaim our hope in the resurrection.

This chapter explains how the Church's funeral rites work when cremation is chosen — what is preferred, what is permitted, and how families can participate in these sacred moments with understanding and peace.

The Three Parts of the Catholic Funeral Rites

The Catholic funeral is not a single event but a journey of prayer, traditionally unfolding in three stages:

1. The Vigil for the Deceased (Wake)
2. The Funeral Mass (or Funeral Liturgy Outside Mass)
3. The Rite of Committal at the cemetery or columbarium

Each part plays an important role in helping the family mourn, pray, and commend the deceased to God's mercy (OCF 45–46).

Cremation After the Funeral Mass: The Church's Strong Preference

Whenever possible, the Church prefers that the body be present for the Funeral Mass, with cremation taking place afterward. This preference exists for several important reasons:

The body is the visible sign of the person.

Seeing the body helps the family acknowledge the reality of death and begin the process of mourning.

The liturgical prayers refer directly to the body.

The sprinkling with holy water recalls baptism. Incense honors the body as a temple of the Holy Spirit. These gestures are deeply meaningful when the body is present.

The presence of the body honors the dignity of the person.

It allows the faithful to pay their respects in a way that mirrors the burial of Christ Himself (OCF 129–130).

When circumstances make this impossible, the Church still allows a Funeral Mass with the cremated remains present.

The Vigil for the Deceased (Wake)

The Vigil is usually held in the funeral home, the church, or a chapel. It is the first moment of public prayer for the deceased.

During the Vigil:

- Scripture is proclaimed
- The family and community pray together
- Stories, memories, and expressions of love are shared
- A Rosary or other devotions may be prayed
- The body (or the cremated remains, if necessary) is honored

This gathering helps the family begin their journey of grieving, supported by faith and community (OCF 54–55).

The Funeral Mass

The Funeral Mass is the central liturgy of the Catholic funeral rites. It is a powerful expression of our faith in Christ's victory over death.

During the Mass:

- The Church prays for the soul of the deceased
- The family is consoled by the Word of God
- The Eucharist is offered — the sacrifice of Christ, who conquers death
- The priest commends the soul to God's mercy

If cremated remains are present:

- They are placed in a simple, dignified urn
- The urn is treated with the same reverence as a body
- It is given a place of honor
- The same prayers of the Mass are offered

The Mass is a profound moment of grace, healing, and hope for the family.

The Final Commendation

At the end of the Funeral Mass, the priest prays the Final Commendation, entrusting the deceased to God's care. The ritual includes:

- Incense as a sign of honor
- A prayer for eternal life
- A solemn expression of faith in the resurrection

This moment marks the beginning of the transition from mourning to hope.

The Rite of Committal

The funeral rites end at the cemetery or columbarium with the Rite of Committal — a simple, solemn act of placing the body or cremated remains in their final resting place.

During this rite:

- The priest or deacon leads prayers
- Scripture is proclaimed
- The grave or niche is blessed (if not blessed previously)
- The remains are interred
- The family receives words of comfort and hope

The Rite of Committal is quiet and intimate, but profoundly meaningful. It is here that families truly entrust their loved one to God (OCF 204–215).

Why the Funeral Rites are Important

The funeral rites serve several essential purposes:

- To honor the dignity of the deceased
- To pray for the salvation of their soul
- To comfort the family through prayer and community
- To proclaim the hope of the resurrection
- To unite the living and the dead in the Communion of Saints

These rites are not merely tradition — they are moments of real grace.

Even With Cremation, Nothing Is Lost

Families sometimes fear that choosing cremation means losing something sacred. But the Church assures us:

- Every prayer of the funeral rites still applies
- Every gesture of honor remains meaningful
- Every hope of the resurrection is unchanged

What matters most is that the cremated remains are treated as the body of a child of God and laid to rest in sacred ground.

Looking Ahead

Now that we have explored the funeral rites with cremation, the next chapter will help answer a very practical question:

"How do we choose the right place to inter the cremated remains?"

Chapter 8 will guide you through the options with clarity and compassion.

CHAPTER 8

How to Choose a Proper Interment Option

For families who choose cremation, one of the most important decisions is selecting a proper place of interment. The Church teaches that cremated remains must be buried or entombed in a sacred place — a cemetery, mausoleum, or columbarium — so that the body is honored, the community can pray, and the dignity of the person is preserved.

This chapter explains the available options, the meaning behind each, and how families can choose the place that best reflects their love and faith.

What Makes a Resting Place "Proper" and "Sacred"?

The Church asks that cremated remains be placed in a location that fulfills three essential purposes:

It must be a permanent resting place.

A home is temporary. Sacred ground is enduring.

It must be consecrated or blessed.

A cemetery or columbarium is a place set apart for God.

It must allow the community to pray for the deceased.

A grave or niche is accessible, respectful, and communal.

When remains are placed in such a location, they receive the dignity that the Church believes every human person deserves (CIC, can. 1240; CCC 2300).

Burial in the Ground (Inhumation)

Many families choose to bury the cremated remains in a traditional grave. This option is simple, sacred, and familiar.

Advantages of Ground Burial

- A permanent place that future generations can visit
- The ability to erect a headstone or grave marker
- A sense of connection to family heritage
- Space for multiple family members to be buried together
- A peaceful and prayerful environment

Ground burial honors Catholic tradition while adapting to modern cremation.

How Burial Works with Cremated Remains

Typically:

- The urn is placed in a burial vault or urn vault
- The grave is blessed if not previously consecrated
- A headstone or marker is installed according to cemetery guidelines
- The Rite of Committal accompanies the burial

This option blends tradition with the practical needs of cremation.

Inurnment in a Columbarium Niche

A columbarium is a structure — often indoors or outdoors — containing rows of niches designed specifically for cremation urns (OCF Appendix; USCCB Cremation Guidelines, 2017).

Benefits of a Columbarium

- A peaceful, dedicated place for cremated remains
- A dignified alternative to ground burial
- Often more affordable than full-size grave spaces
- Weather-protected options available
- Personalized bronze or granite niche plaques
- Space-efficient for parishes and cemeteries

Columbaria are becoming a preferred choice for many Catholic families.

The Meaning of a Niche

A niche:

- Provides a sense of sacred enclosure
- Allows families to personalize a memorial plaque
- Places the deceased among other members of the faith community

Some families also appreciate that a columbarium is easy to visit, even in poor weather.

Entombment in a Mausoleum

Some cemeteries offer special areas within mausoleums for urns. These may include:

- Glass-front niches (when permitted)
- Marble or granite-front niches
- Chapel areas within the mausoleum

Why Some Families Choose a Mausoleum

- Indoor climate control
- An enclosed sacred space
- A quiet environment for prayer
- Elevated memorial options

Mausoleums often include artwork, statues, and devotional spaces that enhance the spiritual atmosphere.

Communal Ossuaries in Catholic Tradition

A growing number of Catholic cemeteries offer communal ossuaries — dignified, consecrated spaces where cremated remains may be interred together while still receiving the full honor of Catholic burial. Although less familiar to many families, the ossuary reflects ancient Christian practice: placing the faithful departed in a sacred resting place where their memory is preserved, their dignity upheld, and their hope in the resurrection proclaimed.

An ossuary is not a place of anonymity. It is a **communal tomb**, blessed by the Church, where the names of the deceased are recorded and memorialized. Families often appreciate that an ossuary offers a reverent and economical option while still fulfilling every requirement of Catholic burial. The Church teaches clearly that cremated remains must be laid to rest in a sacred place — a cemetery, mausoleum, columbarium, or other consecrated structure — as a sign of faith and respect (CIC, can. 1176 §3; CCC 2300; *Ad resurgendum cum Christo*, 5).

Why Some Families Choose an Ossuary

For many families, a communal ossuary provides meaningful advantages:

- **A Permanent Resting Place**
  The ossuary is a stable, enduring location where the faithful can be remembered and prayed for. Even though the remains are placed together, the Church ensures that each person's name is preserved with dignity.
- **A Sacred and Affordable Option**
  Because ossuaries serve multiple families, they often reduce the financial burden while still providing a thoroughly Catholic burial option. Cost should never prevent a family from

choosing what the Church asks for their loved one — interment in holy ground.
- **A Continuation of Ancient Christian Practice**
Early Christians commonly used shared tombs and burial chambers, emphasizing unity in Christ and hope in the resurrection. An ossuary echoes these traditions by gathering the faithful departed into a single sacred space (cf. CIC, can. 1180).
- **A Place for Prayer and Remembrance**
Every Catholic burial place — whether grave, niche, mausoleum, or ossuary — is a place of prayer. The ossuary invites families to visit, pray, and commend their loved ones to God alongside the whole Christian community.

How Interment in an Ossuary Takes Place

Interment in an ossuary typically involves:

- Placing the cremated remains, usually in a biodegradable or minimal container, into the communal chamber
- Recording the name of the deceased in a permanent memorial register
- Offering the **Rite of Committal**, just as at any Catholic burial (OCF, Rite of Committal)
- Entrusting the person to God within the communion of saints

Even when remains are commingled, the Church's teaching is clear: the dignity of the human person is never lost, and the body — even in cremated form — must always be treated with reverence (CCC 364–365; *Ad resurgendum cum Christo*, 6).

The Theology Behind an Ossuary

A Catholic ossuary expresses a profoundly Christian truth: **the dead are never isolated — they rest among the faithful, awaiting the resurrection.**

In a world that sometimes treats death as merely practical or private, the communal ossuary affirms that every person belongs to the Church, both in life and in death. Just as Christian burial proclaims our unity in Christ, so too does a shared resting place testify that *no one is forgotten, and no one journeys alone.*

For families who desire a reverent, faithful, and meaningful resting place for their loved one, the ossuary is a beautiful expression of the Church's love and hope — a place where the departed are entrusted to God, surrounded by the prayers of the whole Christian community.

Family Tombs or Estate Lots

In some regions, especially in areas with a strong Catholic heritage, families have:

- Above-ground tombs
- Family vaults
- Estate sections within cemeteries

Cremated remains may be placed within these family spaces, keeping generations together (CIC, can. 1180).

This Option Honors Family Unity

Families who value generational continuity often prefer:

- A shared resting place
- A prominent memorial structure
- Clear continuity for family lineage

This option preserves a strong sense of belonging and history.

Choosing an Urn: Beauty, Simplicity, and Dignity

The Church does not require elaborate urns. What matters most is that the urn is:

- Dignified
- Secure
- Appropriate for burial or entombment

Families often choose:

- Wood
- Metal
- Marble
- Stone
- Ceramic

Simple, elegant designs reflect Christian humility and respect.

Factors to Consider When Selecting an Interment Option

When deciding among burial, a niche, or a mausoleum, families may consider:

Cost

Columbarium niches may cost less than full burial; mausoleum placements may vary. Cemeteries typically offer a range of price points.

Location

Families often choose a cemetery connected to their parish or where other relatives are buried.

Weather and Accessibility

Indoor mausoleums or columbaria offer comfort during hot, cold, or rainy conditions.

Future Generations

Selecting a place that children and grandchildren can visit fosters prayer and remembrance.

Personal or family traditions

Some families feel more connected to ground burial; others prefer the neat aesthetics of a columbarium.

The Spiritual Meaning Behind Choosing a Resting Place

Choosing a resting place is not merely a logistical decision. It is a spiritual act of love.

When a family selects a space in a cemetery or columbarium, they are saying:

> **"We entrust our loved one to God's care.**
> **We place them among the faithful.**
> **We choose hope over despair, and faith over fear."**

Interment is a visible expression of trust in God's promise of eternal life.

Looking Ahead

Now that families understand the options for proper interment, the next chapter explains how memorialization — headstones, markers, plaques — serves the Christian tradition of remembering, honoring, and praying for the dead.

CHAPTER 9

Memorialization and Catholic Tradition

Cremation does not diminish a person's dignity or their place within the Christian community. Families sometimes worry that cremation means giving up the traditions they associate with burial — headstones, plaques, memorials, and meaningful places of remembrance. But in the Catholic Church, cremation does not take away the beauty of memorialization.

This chapter helps families understand how Catholic tradition calls us to honor the memory of the dead — and why having a permanent memorial is an important part of grieving, praying, and preserving family history.

The Importance of Remembering the Dead

Catholics have always believed in remembering and praying for those who have gone before us. Memorialization is not simply about marking a location — it is about expressing love, gratitude, and faith in the resurrection (2 Maccabees 12:43–46).

Scripture encourages us to remember the dead:

- "It is a holy and wholesome thought to pray for the dead." (2 Maccabees 12:46)
- The Church prays for the dead at every Mass.

- The month of November is dedicated to remembering the faithful departed.

Forgetting someone is painful. Remembering them in a sacred place is healing.

A Memorial Is a Witness of Love and Faith

A memorial — whether a headstone, plaque, or niche marker — has a deep spiritual and human purpose. It:

- Honors the sacred dignity of the person
- Provides a physical place of connection
- Allows future generations to know their family story
- Witnesses to the Christian belief in eternal life
- Encourages ongoing prayer for the deceased

A memorial is a sign that a person lived, was loved, and is remembered.

Cremation Does Not Eliminate Memorial Options

Families sometimes assume that cremation means a simple box with no marker or that cremated remains cannot be buried with a headstone. This is not true.

Cremation still allows for:

- Traditional headstones

- Flat grave markers
- Upright monuments
- Bronze or granite niche plaques
- Family tomb inscriptions
- Mausoleum-front engravings

The memorial can be just as meaningful, personal, and beautiful as with any traditional burial.

Memorialization Helps the Living Heal

A permanent memorial plays an important role in the grieving process.

It gives families a place to visit and pray.

People often feel comforted by returning to the place where their loved one rests.

It creates ritual and rhythm.

Anniversary visits, birthdays, holidays, and All Souls' Day become moments of remembrance and healing.

It offers closure.

Families can say goodbye, entrust their loved one to God, and begin moving from grief to peace.

It prevents the pain of "nowhere to go."

Without a memorial, families can feel lost and disconnected.

A sacred place anchors the memory of the person in love.

Memorialization Preserves Family History

A permanent resting place allows future generations to know where they come from. Grave markers and columbarium plaques become part of a family's story:

- Children can visit grandparents they have never met.
- Great-grandchildren can learn their ancestry.
- Family heritage is physically preserved.

Without a permanent memorial, much of this history is lost.

Memorialization Strengthens the Communion of Saints

Cemeteries and columbaria are holy places because they express a profound Christian truth: the dead remain part of the Church.

Memorializing a loved one in sacred ground:

- Places their memory among other believers
- Allows the whole Church to pray for them
- Connects their life with the prayers of the saints
- Makes their resting place a place of hope and resurrection

A Christian memorial is not simply a marker — it is a proclamation of faith.

How Families Can Personalize a Memorial

The Church encourages families to memorialize loved ones with beauty, dignity, and reverence. Memorials may include:

- Names and dates
- Scripture verses
- Symbols of faith (cross, rosary, dove, fleur-de-lis, sacred hearts)
- Images of saints
- A brief epitaph
- Veterans' emblems
- Family mottos or prayers

These symbols help tell the story of the person's life and faith (CCC 958; OCF 6).

Even Simple Memorials Are Powerful

Not every memorial needs to be elaborate. A simple bronze plaque or modest headstone can be deeply meaningful.

What matters most is *not* size or ornamentation, but:

- The presence of the person in sacred ground
- The public witness of their faith
- The accessibility of a place for prayer
- The continuity of remembrance through generations

Even the simplest memorial becomes a sign of Christian hope.

Looking Ahead

With memorialization explained, the next chapter will address the most common questions families ask about cremation, burial, and Catholic teaching:

> "Can Catholics be cremated?"

> "What if we already scattered ashes?"

> "Does God still raise cremated bodies from the dead?"

> "What do we do if we've kept remains at home for years?"

Chapter 10 provides compassionate, clear answers to these concerns.

CHAPTER 10

Common Questions Families Ask (A Pastoral Q&A Guide)

Families often have sincere and heartfelt questions about cremation, burial, and Catholic teaching. Some of these questions arise from grief, others from confusion or misinformation, and many from a desire to do what is right for their loved one. This chapter provides clear, gentle answers to the most common concerns.

Can Catholics be cremated?

Yes.

The Catholic Church has allowed cremation since 1963, provided that it is not chosen for reasons contrary to the faith, such as denying the resurrection of the body (CIC, can. 1176 – 1177).

Cremation is permitted, but the cremated remains must be interred in a sacred place, such as a cemetery, columbarium, or mausoleum.

Does the Church prefer the burial of the body before cremation?

Yes.

Whenever possible, the Church strongly prefers the body to be present for the Funeral Mass. This allows:

- The full beauty of the sacred rites
- The body is to be honored as a temple of the Holy Spirit
- Family and friends to properly grieve
- The rituals of the Church (sprinkling, incense) to be celebrated as intended

But if circumstances require cremation before the funeral, the Funeral Mass may still be offered with the cremated remains present.

Why can't we keep the ashes at home? We love our family member.

Your love is exactly why the Church wants the remains placed in a sacred resting place.

Keeping remains at home can unintentionally:

- Prolong grief
- Create emotional burdens
- Lead to accidental neglect or loss
- Separate the deceased from the Christian community

Interment offers:

- Peace
- Closure
- A permanent place of prayer
- Protection and dignity for the remains

It is an act of faith, love, and trust in God's care.

Why can't we scatter the ashes? It seems peaceful or symbolic.

The Church prohibits scattering because it:

- Suggests the body "disappears," rather than awaits resurrection
- Removes the remains from the Christian community
- Eliminates any place for prayer or remembrance
- Can unintentionally disrespect the remains
- Often symbolizes beliefs incompatible with Christian hope

Instead, the Church invites families to honor a loved one's favorite places through prayer or memory — without scattering (CDF, Ad resurgendum cum Christo, 7).

What if we already scattered ashes? Are we in trouble?

No one is ever beyond God's mercy.

If scattering was done without knowing the Church's teaching:

- You may speak with a priest or deacon for pastoral guidance
- Pray for the deceased with confidence
- Take comfort in God's understanding and compassion

While the Church cannot "recover" scattered remains, she always offers healing and mercy for the living.

There is no punishment — only an invitation to understanding, healing, and renewed faith.

What if we have had ashes at home for years? What should we do?

This is extremely common.

The Church's message is simple: It is never too late to do the right and holy thing.

Steps you can take:

- Contact your parish or local Catholic cemetery
- Arrange for a respectful, dignified interment
- Celebrate a Rite of Committal or a prayer service
- Create a permanent memorial for your loved one

The Church receives these remains with *great tenderness*.

Does God still raise cremated bodies from the dead?

Absolutely.

God created the entire universe out of nothing. Raising a cremated body is not difficult for Him.

The resurrection is not about God "reassembling particles" — it is about the soul being reunited with a glorified body through His divine power.

Cremation does not prevent the resurrection (CCC 997; CCC 1017).

Is cremation less holy than burial?

No.

When done in accordance with Church teaching — especially with proper interment — cremation is fully consistent with Catholic faith.

What matters is:

- The intention (not rejecting Christian belief)
- The reverent treatment of the remains
- Burial in a sacred place

Holiness comes from love, faith, and the hope of resurrection.

Does burial cost more than cremation?

Not necessarily. Many Catholic cemeteries offer cremation burial options that are:

- Affordable
- Dignified
- Permanent
- Compatible with Church teaching

Columbarium niches often cost less than full-sized graves. Simple grave markers can also be affordable. Your parish or cemetery can help you explore options.

What if our family disagrees about what to do with the remains?

This is a common situation. Here are helpful steps:

- Pray together
- Speak with a priest or deacon
- Learn what the Church teaches and why
- Base decisions on faith, not convenience
- Remember that the goal is to honor the loved one

Interment protects the dignity of the remains and resolves confusion among descendants.

Can we divide the ashes so each family member has some?

No.

The Church teaches that the remains must be kept together because they represent the body of a single person.

Dividing remains:

- Fragments the dignity of the body
- Blurs the sacred meaning of funeral rites
- Causes complications for future generations

Keeping the remains intact respects the integrity of the person.

What kind of urn should we choose?

The Church does not require anything elaborate.
The urn should be:

- Dignified
- Secure
- Appropriate for burial or placement in a niche

Simple, beautiful, and respectful is perfect.

Can we have a memorial service after the burial?

Yes.

Families may celebrate:

- Memorial Masses
- Rosaries
- Votive candles
- Graveside prayers
- Anniversary or All Souls' Day visits

Interment does not end remembrance — it begins it.

Looking Ahead

Having answered the most common questions families ask, the next chapter will guide those who currently have cremated remains at home or have not yet arranged for a proper burial.

CHAPTER 11

Bringing Cremated Remains to the Church for Proper Interment

Many families today have cremated remains stored at home — in a bedroom, closet, office, attic, or even in a drawer. This is almost always done out of love, grief, or uncertainty. Some families inherited cremated remains, but they didn't know how to handle them. Others held onto them because the pain of loss was too great at the time. Some simply didn't realize that the Church requires the remains to be interred.

Whatever the reason, the Church's message is always the same:

It is never too late to do the right and holy thing.

This chapter will guide you through simple, compassionate steps to provide a sacred resting place for your loved one (OCF 204).

A Message of Mercy and Welcome

The Church does not judge families who kept remains at home out of love. There is no shame, no guilt, and no criticism.

Instead, the Church invites families to experience healing by returning the remains to sacred ground. Burial is an act of faith and closure — not a correction of past mistakes.

Your loved one deserves dignity. You deserve peace.

Why This Step Matters

Bringing cremated remains for proper interment:

- Honors the sacred dignity of the person
- Proclaims your faith in the resurrection
- Lifts emotional and spiritual burdens
- Provides a permanent place of prayer
- Protects the remains for future generations
- Allows the Church to accompany you in grief

It is a moment of grace — not an obligation.

How to Begin the Process

Starting is easier than most families expect. Here are the simple steps:

Step 1: Contact Your Parish or Catholic Cemetery

Call your parish office, pastor, deacon, or cemetery staff and explain that you have cremated remains at home and would like to arrange for proper interment. You will be welcomed warmly.

Step 2: Schedule Time to Meet

You can meet with:

- A priest
- A deacon
- The cemetery director or staff
- A pastoral minister

They will help guide you through your options (CIC, can. 1180 – 1181).

Step 3: Select a Resting Place

You may choose:

- A burial plot
- A columbarium niche
- A mausoleum placement
- A family tomb

Cemetery staff can help you find an option that fits your needs, preferences, and budget.

Step 4: Bring the Urn to the Church or Cemetery

On the day of interment, simply bring the urn in a dignified manner. If the urn is temporary, the staff can help transfer the remains to a permanent urn.

Step 5: Celebrate the Rite of Committal

A priest or deacon will pray the Church's beautiful burial prayers. This simple, sacred moment is often deeply healing for families.

What If the Urn Is Stored in a Box or Old Container?

Do not worry. This is extremely common.

The remains will be treated with full dignity, even if:

- The urn is old
- The container is temporary
- The ashes are in the original plastic bag
- The family never transferred the remains

Cemetery staff can assist with the reverent handling and transfer of the remains.

What If We Don't Know What the Deceased Wanted?

Many families struggle with this. The Church's guidance is simple:

Provide the most dignified, faithful option available now.

Interment is always the right choice, even if the person did not leave specific instructions. Burial in sacred ground honors both God and the person's memory.

What If We Don't Have the Funds?

Most Catholic cemeteries and parishes:

- Offer affordable cremation niches or burial plots
- Provide payment plans or assistance
- Have spaces reserved specifically for cremated remains
- Will work compassionately with families
- Never turn someone away for lack of resources

Do not let financial concerns prevent you from contacting the parish or cemetery.

What to Expect Emotionally

Families are often surprised by the emotions they feel during this process. These may include:

- Relief
- Gratitude
- Peace
- Closure
- A sense of "rightness"
- Renewed connection with God and the Church

Interment can be one of the most healing moments in the entire journey of grief.

Preparing the Family

If multiple family members are involved, consider:

- Explaining the Church's teaching gently
- Emphasizing the dignity of burial
- Reassuring relatives that this is an act of love
- Involving children, if appropriate
- Choosing an inscription or a memorial prayer together

The burial can become a unifying moment for the entire family.

Honoring the Person After Interment

Interment is not the end of remembrance — it is the beginning.

Families can continue to honor their loved one by:

- Visiting the grave or niche
- Praying on anniversaries and special dates
- Lighting candles on All Souls' Day
- Requesting Mass intentions
- Bringing flowers or memorial offerings

A sacred resting place allows these gestures to flourish.

The Church Walks With You

No family must take this step alone. Your parish and cemetery are ready to:

- Pray with you
- Offer comfort

- Help you find a resting place
- Assist with the liturgy
- Support your grief
- Welcome your loved one home

The Church accompanies every family with gentleness and love.

Looking Ahead

The final chapter will draw together the meaning of everything presented in this booklet and offer families a concluding message of hope, faith, and consolation.

CHAPTER 12

Conclusion: A Final Word of Faith, Hope, and Love

The death of someone we love is one of the most painful experiences we will ever face. Nothing prepares the heart for the emptiness, longing, and sorrow that follow the loss of a spouse, parent, child, relative, or friend. Yet in the midst of this grief, the Catholic Church offers something the world cannot give: the promise that death has been conquered, and we shall live again in Christ.

Throughout this booklet, we have reflected on the Church's beautiful and ancient teachings about the human body, the dignity of the deceased, the resurrection of the dead, and the sacred duty of burial. These teachings flow not from rules, but from love — God's love for His people, and the Church's love for every soul entrusted to her care.

We Honor the Body Because God Honored It First

The human body is not disposable. It is not a shell. It is not something to disregard once the soul has departed. It is the body through which a person loved, believed, prayed, laughed, suffered, and lived. It is the body that was washed in baptism, anointed with sacred chrism, and nourished with the Eucharist. It is the body that God Himself will raise up in glory on the last day (CCC 364 – 365; CCC 2300).

To inter cremated remains in sacred ground is to affirm this truth: The body matters — now and forever.

We Choose Burial Because We Believe in the Resurrection

Christ Himself was buried. His tomb — once a place of sorrow — became the birthplace of hope. Every Catholic grave, every columbarium niche, every mausoleum crypt echoes this mystery: Here rests a child of God, awaiting the resurrection promised by Christ (1 Corinthians 15:51–55; John 6:39 – 40).

When we bury our loved ones, we proclaim that death does not have the final word. Love does. Grace does. Jesus does.

We Place the Dead in Sacred Ground Because No One Journeys Alone

A cemetery is not a place of abandonment — it is a place of belonging. The faithful departed rest not in isolation, but in the communion of saints, surrounded by the prayers of the Church and the love of Christ.

To bury cremated remains is to give them a home among the faithful…

> **where their memory is cherished,**
> **their dignity protected,**
> **and their legacy preserved for generations.**

We Entrust Our Loved Ones to God Because He Is Faithful

Interment is not an act of letting go — it is an act of handing over. It is a prayer whispered through tears:

> **"Lord, receive them. Keep them. Raise them up."**

God is faithful. He does not abandon His children in life — or in death.

A Final Word to Families

If you have lost someone you love, know this:

> **The Church holds you close.**
> **Christ walks with you.**
> **Your loved one rests in the heart of God.**

If you have cremated remains at home, or if decisions were made in a time of grief or confusion, know that it is never too late to choose a sacred and beautiful resting place. The Church welcomes you with tenderness and joy as you take this step of faith.

You are not alone.
Your grief is seen.
Your love is honored.
The entire Body of Christ shares your hope.

May this booklet guide you, comfort you, and give you peace as you honor the life of someone you hold dear.

A Concluding Prayer

Heavenly Father,
source of all comfort and hope,
we entrust to Your mercy those we love who have gone before us in faith.
Grant them eternal rest and let perpetual light shine upon them.

Give us strength in our grief,
peace in our hearts,
and trust in the promise of resurrection.
May we honor the bodies of our loved ones with dignity,
laying them to rest in sacred ground,
as we await the day when You make all things new.

Through Christ our Lord. Amen.

GENERAL INDEX

A

Afterlife, Christian belief in 7–11, 69–70
All Souls' Day 12, 33, 40, 60, 61
Ashes, handling of 17–18, 22, 29–36, 39–41

B

Baptism, meaning of 6, 11
Body, dignity of 1, 5–8, 11, 16–18, 22
Burial, Catholic requirement for 9–13, 16–21, 22–27, 49–55
Burial, importance of sacred ground 11–13, 22–27, 49–50

C

Canon Law (CIC) references 15–16, 23, 30, 49, 53–55, 75
Cemetery, role of 11–13, 23–27, 33, 38, 49–50
Church teaching, foundations of 1–4, 5–8, 15–21
Closure, role of burial in 25–27, 31–34
Columbarium 18, 23, 49–52
Communion of Saints 12, 26, 47, 62
Cremation, Church teaching on 15–21, 65–72

D

Death, Catholic understanding of 5–11
Dignity of remains 1, 5–8, 16–18, 22–25

E

Eternal life, Christian hope in 7–11, 69–70, 81–82
Evangelization through burial witness 27, 49, 62

F

Family history and memorialization 23, 49–50, 61–63
Funeral Mass with cremation 17–18, 44–45
Funeral Rites, structure of 18, 43–47

G

Grave, role of 11–13, 22–27, 33, 49–51
Grief, healing process 7, 25–27, 31–35, 61, 77–78

H

Home retention of remains 18, 29–36, 66–68
Human person, theology of 1, 5–8, 11

I

Interment, reasons for 16–27, 31–36, 49–58
Introduction to Church teaching... 1–4
Instruction *Ad resurgendum cum Christo*.................... 4, 16–18, 22–25, 37–40

J

Jesus Christ, example of burial 6, 10

K

Keeping remains at home, concerns about.................... 18, 29–36, 66–68

L

Legacy, family remembrance.. 23, 49–50, 61–63
Liturgical meaning of burial 10–13, 18, 43–47

M

Memorialization 23, 49–50, 59–63
Mourning, pastoral support..7, 25–27, 31–35, 65–68

N

Niches (columbaria) 18, 49–52

O

Ossuary..53–55
Order of Christian Funerals (OCF) references .12, 17–18, 23, 26, 43–47

P

Prayer for the dead 12, 23, 40, 60–62
Purification of grief 25–27, 31–34

Q

Questions, common pastoral 65–72

R

Resurrection of the body 1, 6–11, 16, 22–23, 37–40, 69–70
Rite of Committal 18, 26–27, 46, 75

S

Sacred ground	11–13, 22–27, 49–50
Sacredness of the body	1, 5–8, 11, 16–18
Scattering cremated remains	18, 22–25, 37–42
Scripture references	6–7, 9–11, 22–23, 59–60
Sorrow and Christian hope	7–11, 69–70, 81–82

T

Tradition, Catholic burial	9–13
Tombs, family	12–13, 55–56

U

Urns, selection of	17–18, 56, 71
Unity of the Church with the dead	12, 26, 47, 62

V

Visitation, importance of grave/niche	12, 23, 33, 49–52

W

Why interment matters	16–27
Witness to faith through burial	27, 49, 62

www.ingramcontent.com/pod-product-compliance
Lightning Source LLC
Chambersburg PA
CBHW070450050426
42451CB00015B/3426